Creating God's Family In Christmas

An Advent Service
For All Ages

Cynthia E. Cowen

CSS Publishing Company, Inc., Lima, Ohio

ISBN 0-7880-1053-0

As a wife, mother, mother-in-law, daughter, daughter-in-law, sister, sister-in-law, and aunt, I have many roles in a defined family. I also have an extended role in the community of faith, the family of God. I have been truly blessed to be a part of a loving blood family and the extended family in Christ I serve and live with.

I dedicate this book to my immediate family: my husband Stephen, who encourages and supports my writing ministry; my sons Nathan and Justin, who have been blessings to us both; my new daughter-in-law Melissa, whom I have embraced as the daughter I never had; and to all the members of the Cowen and Apelgren family who witness to their faith in Jesus by their participation in the life of the church.

To my friends and to the faithful who gather each Christmas to honor the Christ Child, I pray God's blessings.

May this resource bless all who use it as you celebrate with me our oneness in the family of God.

Cynthia E. Cowen

Table Of Contents

Bulletin

Creating God's Family In Christmas

*Call To Worship

Leader

*Congregational Hymn: "Prepare The Royal Highway"

The World Family Of God

Leader

Grade 6: "Joy To The World" (v. 1)

The Family Of The Light

Leader

Reader: John 1:1-9

Leader

Congregational Hymn: "Good Christian Friends, Rejoice"

The Historical Family Of Israel

Leader

Reader: Luke 2:1-3

Leader

Congregational Hymn: "Oh, Come, Oh, Come, Emmanuel" (vv. 1 and 5)

The Davidic Family

Leader

Reader: Luke 2:4-5

Grade 1: "O Little Town Of Bethlehem" (vv. 1 and 2)

Leader

Congregational Hymn: "O Little Town Of Bethlehem" (vv. 3 and 4)

Our Response To Being Family

Leader

Offering and Special Music

A Family Of God's Creatures

Leader

Congregational Hymn: "Infant Holy, Infant Lowly" (vv. 1 and 2)

Grades 4 and 5: "The Friendly Beasts"

Leader

Congregational Hymn: "Oh, Come, All Ye Faithful" (vv. 1 and 2)

The Family Of Joseph And Mary

Leader

Congregational Hymn: "Go Tell It On the Mountain" (vv. 1 and 3)

The Holy Family

Leader

Reader: Luke 2:6-7

Leader

Pre-K and Kindergarten: "Away In A Manger" (vv. 1-3)

Leader

Congregational Hymn: "What Child Is This?" (vv. 1-3)

The Angelic Family

Leader

Congregational Hymn: "As With Gladness Men Of Old" (vv. 1 and 2)

Leader

Congregational Hymn: "Angels, From The Realms Of Glory" (vv. 1 and 2)

Leader

Reader: Luke 2:13-14

Grade 2: "Angels We Have Heard On High" (v. 1)

Leader

Congregational Hymn: "O Holy Night" (v. 1)

The Lowly Shepherd Family

Leader

Congregational Hymn: "It Came Upon The Midnight Clear" (vv. 1 and 2)

Leader

Reader: Luke 2:8-11

Grade 3: "The First Noel" (vv. 1 and 2)

Leader

Reader: Luke 2:16-18

Leader

Congregational Hymn: "It Came Upon The Midnight Clear" (vv. 3 and 4)

Leader

Congregational Hymn: "O Come, Little Children" (vv. 1-3)

God's Faithful Family In Christ

Leader

***Congregational Hymn:** "Silent Night, Holy Night" (vv. 1-3) Congregation and Youth

***Leader**

Benediction

Leader: Go in the name of the Father, the Son, and the Holy Spirit. Go as members of God's faithful family, rejoicing in the birth of the Christ Child.

All: Amen.

***Congregational Hymn:** "Hark! The Herald Angels Sing" (vv. 1-3)

Creating God's Family In Christmas

*Call To Worship

Leader: Today we, the family of God, gather to celebrate and to announce that a Messiah has been born; a King has been given to us. As we worship the Christ Child, let us join God's heavenly choir giving glory to that newborn King. For the Christ Child, born into our midst, announces the reign of God. Jesus is Emmanuel — God with us. Let us prepare the way, for our Messiah comes.

*Congregational Hymn: "Prepare The Royal Highway"

(Grade 6 and readers enter waving palm branches, wearing crowns, led by one carrying a large candle. Readers will remain up front for entire program.)

The World Family Of God

Leader: God's word was fulfilled in Jesus. Christ came to the world's family to reveal God's great love and forgiveness for all his children. What joy awaits us this night! What Good News is announced to the whole world!

Grade 6: "Joy To The World" (v. 1)

The Family Of The Light

Leader: It was dark that first night. Dark because there was no hope. A Messiah was needed. A Savior was longed for. Out of the darkness came a great light. *(Child with candle steps forward.)* A light of hope from a child, the Son of God, who is the Light.

Reader: John 1:1-9

Leader: Now that message should bring joy to all ears. Let us rejoice as God's family with all our heart and soul and voice as we sing verses 1 and 3 of "Good Christian Friends, Rejoice."

Congregational Hymn: "Good Christian Friends, Rejoice" *(Verses 1 and 3 sung as Grade 6 departs, leaving candle and palm by manger.)*

The Historical Family Of Israel

Leader: Christ came into the world to save the world and all who live in it. Jesus entered a point in time, and God arranged to be part of the world's history. Hear of that time.

Reader: Luke 2:1-3

Leader: God moved the Emperor of Rome to take a count of the people in his empire in order to fulfill the prophecy spoken of in Micah 5:2, "But you, O Bethlehem of Ephrathah, who are one of the little clans of Judah, from you shall come forth for me one who is to rule in Israel, whose origin is from of old, from ancient days." God had promised to come to his people, Israel. God had promised to come and dwell with them as Emmanuel, God with us. Let us join in verses 1 and 5 of "Oh, Come, Oh, Come, Emmanuel" as we ask God to be with us.

Congregational Hymn: "Oh, Come, Oh, Come, Emmanuel" *(Verses 1 and 5 sung as Grade 1 enters carrying large keys of David and Bethlehem signs.)*

The Davidic Family

Leader: "Oh, come, O Key of David," our voices sang. God had promised to be with King David and his family. One of his descendants would sit upon the throne as ruler according to that promise. Jesus Christ is from that royal line of David. Jesus is that one we call Emmanuel. Jesus is the one who would be born in a little town called Bethlehem.

Reader: Luke 2:4-5

Grade 1: "O Little Town Of Bethlehem" (vv. 1 and 2)

Leader: And so, Joseph and Mary, both from the line of King David of Israel, were in the right spot, Bethlehem, at the right time, the point of God's entry into our midst. God was about to present a wonderful gift to them and to each of us down through history. Let us continue to sing of that wondrous gift with verses 3 and 4 of "O Little Town Of Bethlehem."

Congregational Hymn: "O Little Town Of Bethlehem" *(Verses 3 and 4 are sung as Grade 1 processes out, leaving a key and a Bethlehem sign.)*

Our Response To Being Family

Leader: As part of the family of God, we are blessed to share our gifts with his body, the church, through our offerings. As we worship the Christ Child by passing our offering plates, let us rejoice in this part of our Christmas response to God's love.

Offering And Special Music

A Family Of God's Creatures

Leader: The little town of Bethlehem was filled because of the census the Emperor decreed. So Mary and Joseph, soon to arrive, would find only a stable to receive them. Among the lowly beasts of that stable a Holy Infant would be born.

13

Congregational Hymn: "Infant Holy, Infant Lowly" *(Verses 1 and 2 sung as Grades 4 and 5 enter dressed as beasts: donkeys, cows, sheep, doves, and camels.)*

Grades 4 and 5: "The Friendly Beasts"

Leader: The Infant Holy would first be adored by the lowly stable animals. Their home, their warmth, their gentle noises, would be the first gifts our Lord would receive. Come, let us adore him.

Congregational Hymn: "Oh, Come, All Ye Faithful" *(Verses 1 and 2 sung as Grades 4 and 5 depart, leaving a donkey, cow, sheep, dove, and camel behind.)*

The Family Of Joseph And Mary

Leader: As the earth lay in slumber, God was about to enter the world and become part of the family of Joseph and Mary. Salvation was about to be born and laid in a manger. The mountains would soon rejoice as that Good News was told everywhere. Let us tell it now by singing verses 1 and 3 of "Go Tell It On the Mountain."

Congregational Hymn: "Go Tell It On The Mountain" *(Verses 1 and 3 are sung as Pre-kindergarten and Kindergarten enter dressed as Marys and Josephs. Girls may carry dolls wrapped in blankets. An adult couple with real baby may also accompany the group.)*

The Holy Family

Leader: Yes, salvation was born that blessed Christmas morn. The little family of two was increased to three. Let us hear of that holy birth.

Reader: Luke 2:6-7

Leader: Mary gave birth to Christ in a stable. She placed the newest member of her family in a manger, a feeding trough for the animals. Christ came humbly that all might come to him. All may enter a lowly manger and all may be received by this child born unto us.

Pre-K and Kindergarten: "Away In A Manger" (vv. 1-3)

Leader: As we come to the manger again this Christmas, let us pause and reflect on the babe, the son of Mary, and his place in our own lives as we sing the words of "What Child Is This?"

Congregational Hymn: "What Child Is This?" *(Verses 1-3 are sung as Pre-Kindergarten and Kindergarten depart, leaving a Mary and Joseph behind with child.)*

The Angelic Family

Leader: That first Holy Night God used pieces from the created universe to announce the birth of his King: a star and an angel. People of that time looked to the stars as signs of God's action in their world. A special Christmas star appeared announcing the birth of the King of Israel. An angel told the shepherds of the birth of the world's King. Upon hearing the Good News, these shepherds raced to see for themselves what had been told to them. As they met Jesus, they bent their knees before their Infant Lord and King. With gladness, let us run to the manger by singing "As With Gladness Men Of Old," verses 1 and 2.

Congregational Hymn: "As With Gladness Men Of Old" *(Verses 1 and 2 are sung as a single angel carries star in.)*

Leader: God sent his messengers that night to declare Christ's birth. These angels, who had been with God at the time of creation and voiced their praise in song, now sang at the birth of Jesus. Let us join them as we continue our worship with the singing of "Angels, From The Realms Of Glory," verses 1 and 2.

Congregational Hymn: "Angels, From The Realms Of Glory" *(Verses 1 and 2 sung as Grade 2 enters dressed as angels.)*

Leader: The angel declaring the Savior's birth was joined with the host of heaven. To all the earth they heralded peace and good will. Hear Luke share that wondrous and welcomed news.

Reader: Luke 2:13-14

Grade 2: "Angels We Have Heard On High" (v. 1)

Leader: On that most holy night, the angels proclaimed, "Glory to God!" Let us remember that night as our angels return to their heavenly home as we sing the first verse of "O Holy Night."

Congregational Hymn: "O Holy Night" *(Verse 1 sung as Grade 2 departs, leaving one angel and star.)*

The Lowly Shepherd Family

Leader: While Mary cradled the Holy Infant, shepherds stood watch over their flocks. These shepherds would now hear the news about the one who would become their Good Shepherd. The world's stillness would be broken with a midnight proclamation.

Congregational Hymn: "It Came Upon The Midnight Clear" *(Verses 1 and 2 sung as Grade 3 enters dressed as shepherds.)*

Leader: Hear what happened that night to this family of shepherds who were abiding in the fields watching over their flocks.

Reader: Luke 2:8-11

Grade 3: "The First Noel" (vv. 1 and 2)

Leader: God gave the gift of Christ, Emmanuel, to the world. Never again would the world be the same. Love, hope, and peace were born unto us and given to us in this Holy Shepherd. Hear now the response of the shepherds.

Reader: Luke 2:16-18

Leader: The shepherds went back into the world to witness to others what they had found in that stable. As we look to the heavens this Christmas night, let us give back the song which the angels joyously sang as we adore God with verses 3 and 4 of "It Came Upon The Midnight Clear."

Congregational Hymn: "It Came Upon The Midnight Clear" *(Verses 3 and 4 sung as Grade 3 departs, leaving a shepherd behind.)*

Leader: And so this Christmas, as you have gathered as a family in Christ to worship, remember to make Christ a part of your life. Remember those of the world who would herald the Child who brought light into our darkness. Remember how history was changed as Bethlehem, the City of David, became the center of an event that changed the world. Recall the Holy Family of Mary, Joseph, and the Christ Child, Jesus. Then join the shepherds, the angels, the beasts, and all of humankind in welcoming the Christ Child into our world once more. Let us now welcome our children back for a song of meditation and praise as we sing three verses of "O Come, Little Children."

Congregational Hymn: "O Come, Little Children" *(Verses 1-3 are sung as all the children return.)*

17

God's Faithful Family In Christ

Leader: As God's family in Christ, let us now join in remembering that special night as Jesus came and united all of us into the one family of God as we sing "Silent Night, Holy Night." Let us rise.

*Congregational Hymn: "Silent Night, Holy Night" (vv. 1-3) *(Congregation and children all join in singing. Lights may be dimmed and candles used in congregation.)*

*Leader: And in Bethlehem, David's royal city, Jesus Christ was born to Mary. God left his throne in heaven and came down to earth to a stable. In a baby born of poor parents and in low estate, we find our Savior holy. That Child, so dear and gentle, is the Lord of heaven and earth. As our final benediction, let us go forth giving glory to the newborn king.

*Benediction

Leader: Go in the name of the Father, the Son, and the Holy Spirit. Go as members of God's faithful family, rejoicing in the birth of the Christ Child.

All: Amen.

*Congregational Hymn: "Hark! The Herald Angels Sing" *(Verses 1-3 are sung as all children and nativity figures depart.)*

Creating God's Family In Christmas

Congregational Hymn: "Prepare The Royal Highway"
(Grade 6 and readers enter.)

Readers
An appropriate number of readers may be selected from junior high students or from Grade 6. Selections may be divided among those selected. The readers will process with the first group and remain up front throughout the whole program.

Grade 6
Props: Carry palm branches and wear crowns. One student carries a large candle. A palm branch may be placed in the manger when the group leaves, as well as a crown. Candle may be placed on a stand to the side.
Song: "Joy To The World" (v. 1)

Reader: John 1:1-9

Congregational Hymn: "Good Christian Friends, Rejoice" (vv. 1 and 3)
(Grade 6 departs, leaving candle and palm by manger.)

Reader: Luke 2:1-3

Congregational Hymn: "Oh, Come, Oh, Come, Emmanuel" (vv. 1 and 5)
(Grade 1 enters.)

Reader: Luke 2:4-5

Grade 1
Props: Make large keys of David and Bethlehem signs. One key and sign can be placed on a backdrop or appropriate area of stable area when leaving.
Song: "O Little Town Of Bethlehem" (vv. 1 and 2)

Congregational Hymn: "O Little Town Of Bethlehem" (vv. 3 and 4)
(Grade 1 departs, leaving a key and Bethlehem sign.)

Congregational Hymn: "Infant Holy, Infant Lowly" (vv. 1 and 2)
(Grades 4 and 5 enter.)

Grades 4 and 5
Costumes: Dress as beasts: donkeys, cows, sheep, doves, and camels. Masks may be constructed from tag board and words printed and placed on back for use. Begin to build the living creche by leaving one of each animal behind the manger.
Song: "The Friendly Beasts"

Congregational Hymn: "Oh, Come, All Ye Faithful" (vv. 1 and 2)
(Grades 4 and 5 depart, leaving a donkey, cow, sheep, dove and camel behind.)

Congregational Hymn: "Go Tell It On The Mountain" (vv. 1 and 3)
(Pre-Kindergarten and Kindergarten enter.)

Reader: Luke 2:6-7

Pre-Kindergarten and Kindergarten
Costumes: Dress as Marys and Josephs. Girls may carry dolls wrapped in blankets. A Mary with doll and Joseph will remain behind. An adult couple with real baby may accompany the group and remain behind instead of youth.

Song: "Away In A Manger" (vv. 1-3)

Congregational Hymn: "What Child Is This?" (vv. 1-3)
(Pre-Kindergarten and Kindergarten depart, leaving a Mary and Joseph behind.)

Congregational Hymn: "As With Gladness Men of Old" (vv. 1 and 2)
(Single angel enters carrying a star.)

Congregational Hymn: "Angels, From The Realms Of Glory" (vv. 1 and 2)
(Grade 2 enters.)

Reader: Luke 2:13-14

Grade 2
Prop: A single angel enters with star.
Costumes: Dress as angels. A single angel and star stay behind.
Song: "Angels We Have Heard On High" (v. 1)

Congregational Hymn: "O Holy Night" (v. 1)
(Grade 2 departs, leaving 1 angel and a star by the stable.)

Congregational Hymn: "It Came Upon The Midnight Clear" (vv. 1 and 2)
(Grade 3 enters.)

Reader: Luke 2:8-11

Grade 3
Props: May carry staffs.
Costumes: Dress as shepherds. A shepherd stays behind.
Song: "The First Noel" (vv. 1 and 2)

Reader: Luke 2:16-18

21

Congregational Hymn: "It Came Upon The Midnight Clear" (vv. 3 and 4)
(Grade 3 departs, leaving a shepherd behind.)

Congregational Hymn: "O Come, Little Children" (vv. 1-3)
(All children return to the front.)

All: "Silent Night, Holy Night" (vv. 1-3)

* If candlelight is desired for this final song, candles should be distributed before the program. It is unwise to have young children up front holding lighted candles. Lights may be dimmed for effect.

Congregational Hymn: "Hark! The Herald Angels Sing" (vv. 1-3)

www.ingramcontent.com/pod-product-compliance
Lightning Source LLC
Chambersburg PA
CBHW071812020426

42331CB00008B/2472